Match It !

A COLLECTION OF INDEX CARD GAMES FOR LEARNERS OF ENGLISH

Sharon Elwell

Raymond C. Clark

PRO LINGUA ASSOCIATES

Pro Lingua Associates, Publishers
P.O.Box 1348
Brattleboro, Vermont 05302- 1348 USA
Office: 802 257 7779
Orders: 800 366 4775
E-mail: prolingu@sover.net
Webstore: www.ProLinguaAssociates.com
SAN: 216-0579

At Pro Lingua
our objective is to foster
an approach to learning and teaching that we call
interplay, *the **inter**action of language*
learners and teachers with their materials,
with the language and culture,
and with each other in active, creative,
*and productive **play.***

Copyright © 2000, 2005 by Sharon Elwell
ISBN 0-86647-132-4

This book was designed and set by Arthur A. Burrows.
It was printed and bound by Capital City Press in Montpelier, Vermont.

Printed in the United States of America
First printing 2005. 3,700 copies.

Contents

Contents

Introduction

Match It! is a collection of index card games for learners of English. It is based on the game "Matched Pairs" from Pro Lingua Associates' *Index Card Games for ESL.* "Matched Pairs" is, in turn, based on the popular game *Concentration.*

There are two basic purposes for this collection: to explore and develop proficiency with English **vocabulary** and to stimulate **conversation.**

The obvious purpose of vocabulary development is to help students with the **meaning** of English words. However, these games focus on more than the meaning of the words. They focus on **usage,** especially **collocations** — words that co-occur in the larger context of phrases and sentences. In addition to helping students learn the words and their collocates, several of the games also work on **pronunciation**, and a few focus on aspects of **grammar** such as subject-verb agreement and irregular past tense inflections.

The second basic purpose of these games, stimulating conversation, is achieved as the students attempt to find the matches. They talk as the game is played, and when the game is over they continue to talk about the game and the words in it. Because the games are <u>fun</u>, the conversation keeps going naturally.

The games and the cards are very simple, and so they are suitable for learners of virtually all ages, with the possible exception of very young children. They are also appropriate for real beginners, with the exception of learners who are pre-literate. However, even these two groups can enjoy some of the very basic games in Part 1.

The games offer a wide range of challenges, from easy to difficult. In general, beginners will do better with the first three or four parts, while advanced learners will find more challenge with the last three parts.

1

How to Make the Games

This is a photocopyable book. Each game is complete on one page. Here's what you do:

    1. Photocopy the page and cut it up into 24 individual pieces of paper.

    2. Paste these pieces of paper onto 24, 3x5 index cards.

    3. Shuffle the cards well. Lay them out face down. Write the numbers 1 to 24 on the back of the cards. The game is now ready to use.

With larger classes, it may be necessary to break the class into groups and make more than one copy of the game. In this case it is useful to put each copy on a different color of card stock. When the game is completed, the colored copies can easily be kept separate from each other. You can also have your students prepare the cards. This will help them become familiar with the words.

One advantage of using index cards, rather than slips of paper, is that the cards can be kept and used over and over. As each new game is played, the collection grows and becomes a more valuable addition to the materials center.

At the bottom of each page, there are a few notes which may be helpful as you prepare, play, and follow up on the games. For reference purposes, the left column is called column X and the right column is column Y.

With each set of 24 cards, your students can play several games. The basic game is called *Match It!,* but in this book we suggest six variations. We also encourage you to make up your own variations and share them with your colleagues, and let us know about them for the next edition.

How to Play Match It!

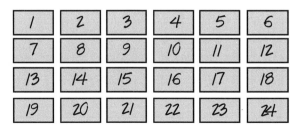

    1. Lay the cards out in a grid. Usually a six-by-four format works best. Place the cards face down with card number 1 at the top left and 24 at the bottom right.

2. In turns, the players call out any two numbers, for example, 6 and 17. The two cards are turned over, and if by chance they match, the player says *"Match!"* and takes the cards. If the cards don't match, they are turned back over with only their numbers showing.

3. As the game progresses, the players struggle to remember the locations and/or numbers of the cards they have seen.

4. The game usually works well with only two or three players. However, it works even better if the players are grouped into teams so that each "player" is a team and has two or three team members cooperating in the search for matches. This arrangement stimulates excited, usually whispered, conversations among the team members as they compare their memories of where the cards are. However, in team play there is a temptation for the students to use their native language, and that, of course, defeats one of the purposes of the game.

5. There are two ways of continuing the play. One way is to allow a player who makes a match to immediately try for another match. However, as the game nears completion, this often allows one player to run away with the game, taking all of the remaining unmatched pairs. To allow for fuller participation, let each player take only one opportunity to make a match, successful or not, and then let the next player take a turn.

6. In **Match It!** and most of the variations of the game, the player must not only make the match, they also need to use the matched words or phrases in sentences. This is an important part of the game

7. There are many possible ways to score these games. The simplest is to give one point for each match. To stress the importance of using the matched words correctly, give one point for a successful match and one point for a successful sentence.

8. In some games more than one possible match may exist. In this case, it is best to go over the pairs before the game is played, so that the "correct" match is identified before play begins. Sometimes two players will disagree on the match. This can lead to some useful discussion, but if it cannot be resolved, you must be the final arbitrator. If several games are going on at the same time, one or more learners can be designated as the arbitrator. In this case, it is useful to give the student arbitrator a full, uncut copy of the game that is being played.

Variations on Match It!

Flash 'n Match

This variation can be done as a main game or as a follow-up to *Match It!*

1. Separate the 24 cards into two stacks. One stack is all the words in column X, and the other stack is the words in column Y.

2. Select one of the columns and carefully show each of the twelve cards to the students. As you show them and put them down face up, you can check that they know the meanings of the words. In some cases, Column X works better, and in some cases, column Y is better.

3. Shuffle the cards in the other column, and then, one by one flash the cards. The students call out the match for the cards. For example, in game 1.6, "oz." is flashed, and the students call out "Ounce!"

4. In a more competitive version, the first student to call out the correct match takes the card. The challenge is to see who can collect the most cards.

Matchmaker

1. All 24 cards are shuffled and put into a single deck, face down.
2. A designated dealer turns over the top cards one at a time.
3. As the cards are turned over, they are placed face up in front of the players, in a row so that each card is visible.
4. Each time the dealer turns over a new card, all the players scan the cards that are already face up. When a player spots a card that will match one of the cards that has been played, they shout *"Matchmaker!"* The first one to shout then says what the match is. If they are correct, they take the two cards. If they are incorrect, another player can attempt a match. If there is no match, the dealer continues.

5. The game may get a little raucous toward the end as everybody tries to be the first to shout, "Matchmaker!" So, after several matches have been made, the dealer can show the new cards to each player in turn and only one player at a time has the opportunity to say, "Matchmaker!"

Challenge Match

1. Divide the class into two teams.

2. Select a game and give one team all the cards from one column and the other team all the cards from the other column.

3. One team begins by putting down a card and challenges the other team to match it. If the match is successful, the team that is challenged keeps the match. If the match is unsuccessful, the challenging team can call out the matching card if they think they know it. If they are successful, they take the matching card.

4. Play continues back and forth until all the cards are matched.

Matchless

This is based on *Go Fish*.

1. There are four players to a game and one complete set of 24 cards.

2. Shuffle the cards and give each player 6 cards.

3. The players check their hands. If they have a match, they call it out, show it, and put it down in front of them. If they're incorrect and another player successfully challenges them, they take the cards back into their hand.

4. Player A, on the dealer's left, begins by asking any other player (player B) for a card that will match one that player A is holding. For example, in game 4.1, player A is holding "Brazil" and asks player B for "Portuguese." If a match is made, player A places the pair in front of them. If player A is unsuccessful, player B says, "Matchless."

5. Successful or not, player A only gets one turn, and the play passes to the player on the left.

6. Play continues until one player has made 6 matches. Alternatively, play continues until all the matches are made.

Category Match

This is similar to the popular TV show *Jeopardy*. The game requires some pre-class preparation.

1. Choose 6 categories (for example, holidays, months, verbs, synonyms, weather, languages).

2. Select 4 cards from one of the columns in each category. In most cases Column X works best.

3. Lay out a grid with the cards face down and the name of the category also on a card, face up, as illustrated below. Down the side put numbers, 1, 2, 3 4.

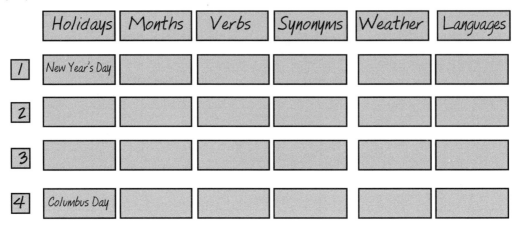

4. As you lay out the grid, try to put the easiest cards along row 1, and the most challenging along row 4. For example, Holidays 1 could be "New Year's Day," and Holidays 4 could be "Columbus Day." You could also try to make row 3 a little harder than row 2.

5. Group the students into two or three teams.

6. One team begins by announcing a category and a number. The dealer turns the card over and the team attempts to make a match with a complete sentence. For example, Holidays One is called out. "New Year's Day" is turned over, and the player says, "New Year's Day is on January first."

7. If the match is successful, the dealer records the points won. This can be done by placing a slip of paper with the player's name on top of or in place of the matched card.

8. Play continues until all the cards are matched. The team with the highest score wins.

Matcho

This game is based on *Bingo*.

Simple Version

1. Divide the class into two or three teams.

2. First, select two games. Separate the 48 cards into one pile from column X and one from column Y. Tell the players which games are being used, for example, irregular past tense, games 2.4 and 2.5.

3. Put all the column X cards (24 total) down in random order, face up on a grid, as indicated below. Put a blank card as the wild card in the very middle square.

M	A	T	C	H
kite flyer	house builder	truck driver	slow runner	beer drinker
fruit seller	meat cutter	walnut grower	bricklayer	catcher
songwriter	diver		grocery buyer	swimmer
storyteller	bell ringer	street sweeper	horn blower	bicycle rider
English teacher	beekeeper	bird feeder	singer	latecomer

4. The dealer shuffles the other deck of 24 column Y cards, draws the top card and calls it out.

5. Team one attempts to find the matching card on the **MATCH** grid. They call out the match and make a sentence. For example:

> ***Dealer:*** Song
>
> ***Team 1:*** (locates the match, "songwriter")
> "Songwriter. Yesterday the songwriter wrote a song."

6. If they are successful, the dealer gives them the card and the card on the grid is turned face down.

7. Play continues until finally one team makes a match that completes a row, column, or diagonal. The team calls out *"Matcho!"*

Matcho • Complex version.

This version of the game requires several copies of the two games so that several grids can be in play at the same time. In this case, when the dealer calls out "song," each player has to make a different sentence when they make the match.

For example:

Dealer:	Song
Player 1:	Yesterday the songwriter wrote a song.
Player 2:	Do you know that the songwriter wrote a new song?
Player 3:	I think the songwriter wrote two new songs.

A Note on Meaning and Usage

The meaning and implications of a few of the collocations, idioms, and proverbs in these games may not be familiar to you, the teacher, and you should be aware that even those you do know may vary around the world and even among regions and age groups in North America. This is particularly true of the idiomatic meaning – the implications of the expressions that may not be clear to you even when you encounter them in context. For example, it is not obvious that the idiom "to bring home the bacon" means to provide support for your family.

Ideally, before using a game in class you would make sure that you fully understand the usage of each phrase, but it is not really necessary for your students to learn the idiomatic usage of all these expressions in order to benefit from the games. It is more important for them to know that we say "bread and butter" and not "butter and bread" than to know what a "bread and butter economic issue" is. However, if you think that your students will want to understand the implications of any specific expression that you are unsure of, we encourage you in preparing your class to consult with colleagues. You will not find such idioms in most dictionaries, but you can also consult one of the excellent dictionaries of American idioms or proverbs available.

1.1 Numbers

1	one
2	two
3	three
4	four
5	five
6	six
7	seven
8	eight
9	nine
10	ten
11	eleven
12	twelve

NOTES: This is a very basic game that simply matches the numeral with its word. A few matters of pronunciation and spelling should be watched. Seven and eleven are the only multisyllable words, and watch for the correct placement of stress. Three and six have the troublesome vowels /iy/ and /i/. Three has the troublesome /th/. When a student makes a match, it would be useful to have them say, "Number one is spelled o–n–e, and pronounced *one*."

BASICS 1

1.2 Numbers

13	30
14	40
15	50
16	60
17	70
18	80
19	90
3	three
3rd	third
33	thirty three
4th	fourth
15th	fifteenth

NOTES: This game will require a little explanation. The teens are matched with the "tys," and the other numbers are matched with their equivalents. There are two pronunciation problems in this game. The first is the difficult -teen/-ty distinction, and the second is the difficult /th/ sound. Because the -teen/-ty distinction is hard to hear, after the match has been made, you could say, "Which one am I saying? I have **thirteen** dollars."

1.3 Symbols

+	plus
−	minus
×	times
÷	divided by
=	equals
>	greater than
<	less than
%	percent
$	dollar
¢	cent
&	and
@	at

NOTES: This is a simple match of common symbols and their spoken and written equivalents. When they make a match, the students could say, "This is the symbol for Y."

BASICS 1

1.4 Arithmetic

20 + 80	100
900 + 100	1000
50 + 60	110
500 – 300	200
90 – 90	0
800 – 400	400
30 × 40	1200
70 × 20	1400
40 × 50	2000
500 ÷ 2	250
600 ÷ 4	150
700 ÷ 350	2

NOTES: This game requires production of numbers mostly in the hundreds. It also requires the students to use the arithmetic terms, so that when they make a match they say, "Twenty plus eighty equals one hundred," etc. Note also that in spoken North American English, *a hundred* is more commonly said than *one hundred*, and *one hundred **and** ten* than *one hundred ten*. When the matching game is over, the cards could be used for a simple flash card game. You flash the card, the students says what's on the card.

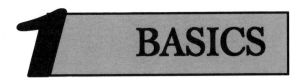

1.5 Measurements A • Linear and Time

in.	inch
ft.	foot/feet
yd.	yard
mi.	mile
mm.	millimeter
cm.	centimeter
m.	meter
km.	kilometer
sq.	square
sec.	second
min.	minute
hr.	hour

NOTES: This game matches abbreviations of linear measurement and time. "Square" may take a little explanation because it is not a linear measurement, although it is often used with *foot, yard, mile*, etc. When a match is made, the student could say, "Y–D is the abbreviation for yard." This game could be coordinated with a lesson on comparative English–metric measurements. Not included are time abbreviations for week, month, and year. You could make these cards and add them to the set.

1.6 Measurements B • Weight and Volume

oz.	ounce
lb.	pound
g.	gram
kg.	kilogram
tsp.	teaspoon
tbsp.	tablespoon
c.	cup
pt.	pint
qt.	quart
gal.	gallon
l.	liter
ml.	milliliter

NOTES: This game matches abbreviations for common measurements for weight and volume. When a match is made, the student can say, "O–Z is the abbreviation for ounce." The game could be coordinated with a lesson on comparative metric–English measurements.

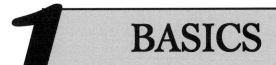

1.7 Months and Ordinals

1/1	Jan. 1st
2/2	Feb. 2nd
3/3	Mar. 3rd
4/4	Apr. 4th
5/5	May 5th
6/6	Jun. 6th
7/7	Jul. 7th
8/8	Aug. 8th
9/9	Sept. 9th
10/10	Oct. 10th
11/11	Nov. 11th
12/12	Dec. 12th

NOTES: This game practices the months of the year, expressions for dates, and ordinal numbers. There are lots of /th/ sounds. It also uses the common abbreviations for the months. When a match is made, the student says, "This is January first. January is the first month of the year." You could also have them spell the month out completely, "J–A–N is the abbreviation for J–A–N–U–A–R–Y."

1.8 Days

Monday	Mon.
Tuesday	Tues.
Wednesday	Wed.
Thursday	Thurs.
Friday	Fri.
Saturday	Sat.
Sunday	Sun.
morning	a.m.
afternoon	p.m.
noon/midnight	12:00
weekend	Sat. & Sun.
weekdays	Mon. – Fri.

NOTES: Abbreviations for days of the week and other time expressions are practiced in this game. This game can be coordinated with lessons on telling time (*at three o'clock*) and days (*on Monday*) and *in the* with *morning, afternoon, evening* and the irregular *at night.*

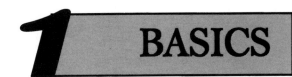

1.9 Time.

9:45	quarter of __
10:05	five past __
10:15	quarter past __
10:30	__ thirty
11:30	half past __
12:00 p.m.	noon
1:15	__ fifteen
2:20	twenty after __
4:45	__ forty five
5:40	twenty to __
6:50	ten to __
12:00 a.m.	midnight

NOTES: Use this game to follow up on telling time. Some of the matches have two possible combinations, for example, 10:30 and 11:30 could be either "half past ten/eleven" or " ten/eleven thirty." This game can be combined with the previous game for a flash card practice. Set up two piles – days and times – and make four more cards: morning, afternoon, evening, and night. In sequence flash *Monday, 10:30, morning,* and the student responds with *"on Monday, at ten-thirty in the morning."*

17

2.1 Doers and Deeds A • Third Person Singular

bird watcher	birds
ballet dancer	ballet
math teacher	math
guitar player	guitar
bike rider	bikes
truck driver	trucks
dog lover	dogs
bread baker	bread
songwriter	songs
violin maker	violins
house painter	houses
firefighter	fires

NOTES: The point of this game is to practice the third person singular verb forms. When the match is made, the student says, "A bird watcher **watches** birds." Also note the pronunciation of **s**. The first three in the list are pronounced /iz/, the second four with the voiced /z/, and the last five with the voiceless /s/.

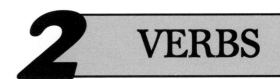

2.2 Doers and Deeds B • Third Person Singular

flower arranger	flowers
movie producer	movies
dog catcher	dogs
window washer	windows
storyteller	stories
food server	food
grape grower	grapes
house cleaner	houses
horse trainer	horses
street sweeper	streets
meat cutter	meat
deer hunter	deer

NOTES: The point of this game is to practice the third person singular verb forms. When the match is made, the student says, "A flower arranger **arranges** flowers." Also note the pronunciation of **s**. The first four in the list are pronounced /iz/, the second five with the voiced /z/, and the last three with the voiceless /s/.

2.3 Doers and Deeds C • Third Person Singular

auto racer	auto
party crasher	parties
dishwasher	dishes
kite flyer	kites
car designer	car
baseball player	baseball
glass blower	glass
bartender	bar
map maker	maps
dog walker	dogs
rubbish collector	rubbish
news reporter	news

NOTES: The point of this game is to practice the third person singular verb forms. When the match is made, the student says, "An auto racer **races** autos." Also note the pronunciation of **s**. The first three in the list are pronounced /iz/, the second five with the voiced /z/, and the last four with the voiceless /s/.

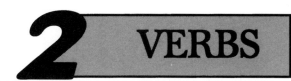

2.4 Irregular Verbs in the Past A

songwriter	song
singer	song
glass blower	glass
beer drinker	beer
bricklayer	bricks
grocery buyer	groceries
walnut grower	walnuts
street sweeper	streets
beekeeper	bees
meat cutter	meat
kite flyer	kite
storyteller	story

NOTES: This game focuses on irregular past tense verbs. When players make a match, they have to begin a sentence with "yesterday" and supply the correct form of the verb. For example, "Yesterday the song writer **wrote** a song." Alternatively, when a match is made, an opposing player says, "What did the songwriter do?"

2.5 Irregular Verbs in the Past B

English teacher	English
truck driver	truck
bicycle rider	bicycle
catcher	baseball
horn blower	horn
latecomer	late
house builder	house
diver	into the pool
bell ringer	bell
slow runner	slowly
fruit seller	fruit
bird feeder	birds

NOTES: This game focuses on irregular past tense verbs. When players make a match they have to begin a sentence with "yesterday" or some other past time expression and supply the correct form of the verb. For example, "Yesterday the English teacher **taught** English." Alternatively, when a match is made, an opposing player says, "What did the English teacher do?" Note that some of the verbs are followed by an adverbial.

2.6 Past Participles

break	broke
choose	chose
eat	ate
forget	forgot
give	gave
know	knew
see	saw
speak	spoke
steal	stole
take	took
throw	threw
wear	wore

NOTES: The students match the present and past forms of these irregular verbs and then say the past participle. They can also say, "Every day I _____; yesterday I _____; and all week I have _____."

2.7 Phrasal Verbs and Object

look up	word
call up	friend
figure out	plan
turn on	TV
look like	mother
pick up	room
throw out	broken thing
look after	children
get out of	commitment
get into	car
get over	illness
do over	homework

NOTES: In addition to matching the phrasal verb with an object, the student should also use a correct determiner (a/n, the, my). Some of these phrasals could have more than one meaning. For example, it would be possible to say, "I'm going to look up an old friend." For that reason, it is best to precede this game with a preview of the intended meanings. Also note that some of these phrasal verbs are separable; the object can come between the two parts of the verb. See if your students can figure this out.

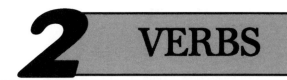

2.8 Verb and Particle

look	at
rely	on
vote	for
escape	from
talk	about
listen	to
cooperate	with
believe	in
vote	for
deal	with
laugh	at
consist	of

NOTES: These verbs are frequently followed by a particle (prepositional form), but they are not phrasal verbs. They take an object, and the object requires a particle (or prepositional phrase). When a match is made, the student should complete the phrase with an appropriate object. Because some of these verbs can take more than one particle, it is best to preview the list. Also note that there are two *at*s and two *with*s.

3.1 Family A

father's wife	mother
son's father	husband
brother's daughter	niece
aunt's husband	uncle
mother's mother	grandmother
parents' son	brother
mother's husband	father
sister's husband	brother-in-law
husband's mother	mother-in-law
sister's son	nephew
uncle's wife	aunt
cousin's father	uncle

NOTES: These matches are made from the female point of view, although the only pair that would be different for a man is "son's father" and "husband." When the match is made, the student should say, "My *x* is my *y*." For example, "My father's wife is my mother." They could also add, if appropriate, "and his/her name is *z*." It might be good to put a family tree diagram on the board as the game is played, and point to the terms as they are matched.

3.2 Family B

children's mother	wife
father's father	grandfather
parents' daughter	sister
aunt's son	cousin
wife's father	father-in-law
brother's wife	sister-in-law
mother's mother	grandmother
wife's brother	brother-in-law
father's new wife	stepmother
stepmother's son	stepson
wife's brother	brother-in-law
brothers and sisters	siblings

NOTES: These matches are made from the male point of view, although the only pair that would be different for a woman is "children's mother" and "wife." When the match is made, the student should say, "My x is my y." For example, "My brother's wife is my sister-in-law." They could also add, if appropriate, "and his/her name is z." It might be good to put a family tree diagram on the board as the game is played, and point to the terms as they are matched.

3.3 Housework

vacuum	carpet
mop	kitchen floor
dust	furniture
mow	lawn
weed	garden
do	dishes
set	table
make	bed
cook	meals
take out	trash
water	plants
feed	cat

NOTES: When a match is made, the students can make a sentence with the pair. Another variation would be for an opposing player to ask, "Have you ever done that?" This would provide some practice of the present perfect with frequency adverbs. For example, "I have often vacuumed the carpet." Some frequency adverbs are *never, rarely, seldom, sometimes, often, usually,* and *always.*

3.4 Getting Ready in the Morning

turn off	alarm
get out of	bed
take	shower
brush	teeth
comb	hair
put on	clothes
eat	breakfast
drink	coffee
read	newspaper
listen to	radio
pack	lunch
lock	door

NOTES: After the students have made all the matches, they can put them together as a natural sequence of events, as indicated above. The sequence could also be practiced with connectors such as *next*, *then*, *after that*, *before*, or *finally*. The sequence could also be done in the past tense. Be sure the students use determiners *(a, the, my)* when they announce a match — they're tricky.

3.5 Weather

foggy	can't see far
raining	umbrella
snowy	ski
windy	sail
cold	coat
sunny	sunbathe
humid	moisture in the air
warm	75°F
hot	90°F
cloudy	no sun
cool	60°F
mild	not hot or cold

NOTES: When these weather terms are matched, the students should say, "When it's X, you need/can,..." or "When it's X, it's/there's ...". Some examples: "When it's foggy, you can't see far;" "When it's raining, you need an umbrella;" "When it's humid, there's moisture in the air;" "When it's mild, it's not hot or cold."

3. 6 Health

salt water gargle	sore throat
aspirin	headache
cast	broken bone
dentist appointment	toothache
911	emergency
ointment	scrape
heating pad	backache
bandage	cut
cough syrup	cough
ice	sprained ankle
antacid	indigestion
nasal spray	stuffy nose

NOTES: When these matches are made, the students could say, "X is good for Y," or "If you have Y, you should (verb) X." For example: "A salt water gargle is good for a sore throat;" "If you have a cough, you should take cough syrup."

3.7 Making a Living

get	job
earn	money
take out	mortgage
open	checking account
make	deposit
balance	checkbook
pay	bills
contribute	charity
join	club
attend	meeting
go	shopping
subscribe	newspaper

NOTES: Because there are multiple possible matches, it is best to go over the intended matches before playing the game. When a match is made, another student could ask, "Why do you earn money?" and the person who made the match has to respond with "I earn money because . . ."

3.8 Holidays

New Year's Day	1/1
Martin Luther King's Day	January
Presidents Day	February
Memorial Day	May
Canada Day	7/1
U.S. Independence Day	7/4
Labor Day	September
Columbus Day	October
Veterans Day	11/11
Thanksgiving	November
Christmas	12/25
Boxing Day	12/26

NOTES: These holiday matches allow the students to practice "in" with months and "on" with days. After the matches have all been made, you could have the students put them in sequence and carry out a little "before and after" game. For example, "When is Canada Day?" "It's after Memorial Day and before Independence Day." Boxing Day is observed in Canada, Great Britain, Australia, and New Zealand. Also note that in Canada, Thanksgiving Day is in October.

3.9 Pockets and Purses

bill	fold
nail	file
bus	token
lip	stick
tooth	pick
credit	card
key	ring
safety	pin
jack	knife
change	purse
driver's	license
cigarette	lighter

NOTES: These are all compound nouns. Note the stress is on the first part of the compound. Some of them are spelled as one word. That can be a challenge to the students. The answers: *billfold, lipstick, toothpick, jackknife.*

4.1 Languages

Portuguese	Brazil
Arabic	Morocco
Hebrew	Israel
Hindi	India
Farsi	Iran
Spanish	Bolivia
German	Austria
Dutch	Netherlands
Swahili	Kenya
French	Canada
Tagalog	Philippines
Catalan	Andorra

NOTES: As the students attempt to make matches, they can be required to use the passive: "X is spoken in Y." To add to the challenge, they can continue the sentence by saying "...by Y(ians, etc.)" If you have students from other countries, make matching cards for them. Be careful of Canada, which is, of course, also English-speaking, but is officially a bilingual country. This can lead to discussion about minority languages such as Kurdish in Iran, Iraq, Syria, and Turkey.

4.2 People

Denmark	Danes
Spain	Spaniards
Norway	Norwegians
Japan	Japanese
Switzerland	Swiss
Italy	Italians
Sweden	Swedes
Costa Rica	Costa Ricans
Dominican Republic	Dominicans
Lebanon	Lebanese
Turkey	Turks
Uzbekistan	Uzbekis

NOTES: The required sentence for making the match is "The people of X are Ys." This could be followed by or alternated with "A person from X is a/n Y." This could lead to adjective forms: "I have never met a/n *Y(-ish, etc.)* person," or something silly like "I'd like to marry a/n *Y(-ish, etc.)* man/woman." You can make cards for your students if their countries are not represented.

4.3 Capitals

Seoul	South Korea
Bangkok	Thailand
Beijing	China
Tokyo	Japan
Islamabad	Pakistan
Ankara	Turkey
Cairo	Egypt
Dakar	Senegal
Warsaw	Poland
Athens	Greece
Bogota	Colombia
Caracas	Venezuela

NOTES: A possible twist on the usual matching procedure: When a student picks up the first card, they have to say either, "I think X is the capital of Y," or "I think the capital of Y is X." If they don't know the answer or give the wrong answer, they can't turn over the second card. If they know, then they pick up the second card looking for a match. You can make cards for your students if their countries are not represented.

4.4 Cities (US and Canada)

Montreal	Quebec
Toronto	Ontario
Calgary	Alberta
Miami	Florida
Houston	Texas
Boston	Massachusetts
Chicago	Illinois
Denver	Colorado
Seattle	Washington
St. Louis	Missouri
Detroit	Michigan
Phoenix	Arizona

NOTES: You may need to precede this game with a geography lesson. If you have a map, you can have the students point to the city or state when they turn over the card. Watch out for the correct placement of stress in these names. For example, chiCAgo, not CHIcago. You can have the students say and identify the syllable with the strongest stress.

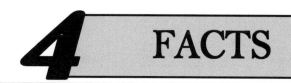

4.5 Land Forms

Sahara	Desert
Rocky	Mountains
Great	Plains
Hawaiian	Islands
Australian	Outback
Russian	Steppes
Grand	Canyon
Florida	Keys
Cape	of Good Hope
Amazon	Basin
Scottish	Highlands
Isthmus	of Panama

NOTES: You may need to precede this game with a geography lesson and definitions of the land forms. After a match has been made, the student has to say, " The XY is/are located in Z." Notice the "of" for "The Isthmus of Panama" and "The Cape of Good Hope." In both cases the geographical term is first in the name. After the matches have been made, collect the cards, shuffle them, and place them in a pile face down. Each student draws a card and attempts to say the other part of the name.

39

4.6 Bodies of Water

Great	Lakes
Indian	Ocean
Yellow	Sea
Hudson	Bay
Persian	Gulf
Suez	Canal
Niagara	Falls
English	Channel
Mississippi	River
St. Lawrence	Seaway
Nile	Delta
Strait	Gibraltar

NOTES: You may need to precede this game with a geography lesson and definitions of the terms for the bodies of water. There are four possibilities for *river*. Tell the students you are using only *Mississippi*. After a match has been made, the student has to say, "(The) XY is/are located in/between/near Y." Notice the irregular *Niagara* and *Hudson* (no *the*) and the required *of* with *Gibraltar*. After the matches have been made, collect the cards, shuffle them, and place them in a pile face down. Each student draws a card and attempts to say the other part of the name. A deck with both the land forms and bodies of water can add to the challenge.

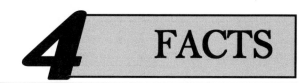 **FACTS**

4.7 Famous People

Albert	Einstein
Indira	Gandhi
Emperor	Hirohito
Mao	Tse Tung
Simon	Bolivar
Abraham	Lincoln
Winston	Churchill
Jomo	Kenyatta
Florence	Nightingale
Marie	Curie
Eleanor	Roosevelt
Queen	Victoria

NOTES: These are all historical figures. When a match is made, the student can be asked to say, "X was a famous Y," or "He/she is known for...," or "X was from Y." Another game could be created using contemporary people. You could ask each student to write a name on index cards – first name on one card, last name on another card. (With a small class the students may need to write more than one each.) Collect the cards, check them over, select 12 pairs (no two names alike), and proceed to play *Match It!*

4.8 Products

Maine	lobster
Vermont	maple syrup
Maryland	crabs
Alaska	salmon
California	wine
Kansas	wheat
Idaho	potatoes
Wisconsin	cheese
Texas	oil
Iowa	corn
Georgia	peaches
Louisiana	shrimp

NOTES: Some of these matches could be debated. For example, Maine is proud of its potatoes. However, that's all part of the fun of playing the game. The matching sentence could be "X(State) is known for its Y," or "Y is a product of/associated with X(State)."

FACTS

4.9 The Zodiac

Aries	3/21 – 4/20
Taurus	4/21 – 5/21
Gemini	5/22 – 6/21
Cancer	6/22 – 7/23
Leo	7/24 – 8/23
Virgo	8/24 – 9/23
Libra	9/24 – 10/23
Scorpio	10/24 – 11/22
Sagittarius	11/23 – 12/21
Capricorn	12/22 – 1/20
Aquarius	1/21 – 2/19
Pisces	2/20 – 3/20

NOTES: This game does not have a strong lexical or linguistic objective, but it does stimulate conversation as the students discover each other's signs. Bring in a horoscope when you play it. It does offer some practice in reading dates in the English order (month first). You could add the English vocabulary for the signs: *ram — bull — twins — crab — lion — virgin — scales — scorpion — archer — goat — water carrier — fish*.

5.1 Opposites • with *-ful* and *-less*

thoughtless	thoughtful
fearless	fearful
careless	careful
hopeless	hopeful
pitiless	pitiful
harmless	harmful
helpless	helpful
useless	useful
meaningless	meaningful
colorless	colorful
joyless	joyful
thankless	thankful

NOTES: The matches are easy to make. To add to the challenge, the students can be required to define the words or use them in a sentence. The game can be followed with an exploration of words that don't have the "-ful/-less" contrast. For example, *defenseless, odorless, peaceful, successful, skillful.*

5.2 Negation A • with *in-*, *im-*, *il-*, *ir-*

sensitive	__sensitive
secure	__secure
capable	__capable
tolerant	__tolerant
patient	__patient
polite	__polite
practical	__practical
possible	__possible
legal	__legal
literate	__literate
regular	__regular
responsible	__responsible

NOTES: The blank before each word in column Y represents one of the *"in-"* prefixes. The trick with these matches is to choose the correct form of the prefix. The form is determined by the pronunciation of the first letter of the word. See if your students can figure it out. *im-* before *p* (also *b* and *m*), *il-* before *l*, *ir-* before *r*. Words beginning with all other letters use *in-*.

5.3 Negation B • with *un-*, *mis-*, *dis-*

sure	__sure
steady	__steady
lucky	__lucky
happy	__happy
fair	__fair
friendly	__friendly
use	__use
spell	__spell
understand	__understand
agreeable	__agreeable
honest	__honest
respectful	__respectful

NOTES: The blank before the words in the Y column represents one of the three negative prefixes, ***un-,*** ***mis-, dis-.*** The challenge to the student is to choose the right one. The students can also be asked to identify the adjectives and verbs (all the ***mis-*** prefixes go with verbs, although ***misuse*** can also be a noun). They can also try to use the words in a sentence. Of the four games of this type, this is probably the easiest, and the fourth game (D), the hardest.

5.4 Negation C • with *un-, mis-, dis-*

important	__important
comfortable	__comfortable
certain	__certain
afraid	__afraid
usual	__usual
inform	__inform
judge	__judge
lead	__lead
courteous	__courteous
pleased	__pleased
loyal	__loyal
respect	__respect

NOTES: The blank before the words in the Y column represents one of the three negative prefixes, *un-, mis-, dis-*. The challenge to the student is to choose the right one. The students can also be asked to identify the adjectives and verbs (all the *mis-* prefixes go with verbs). They can also try to use the words in a sentence.

5.5 Negation D • with *un-, mis-, dis-*

concerned	__concerned
selfish	__selfish
reliable	__reliable
pleasant	__pleasant
popular	__popular
common	__common
pronounce	__pronounce
treat	__treat
behave	__behave
like	__like
trust	__trust
ability	__ability

NOTES: The blank before the words in the Y column represents one of the three negative prefixes, *un-, mis-, dis-*. The challenge to the student is to choose the right one. The students can also be asked to identify the adjectives and verbs. In this game, *dis-* occurs with verbs (*trust* and *like*) and a noun (*ability*). Also note that *like* and *able* can also be used with *un-*. For that reason, it would be best to preview the game. The students can also try to use the words in a sentence.

5.6 Negation E • with *un-, mis-, dis-*

predictable	__predictable
avoidable	__avoidable
ashamed	__ashamed
sympathetic	__sympathetic
neighborly	__neighborly
dependable	__dependable
interpret	__interpret
place	__place
represent	__represent
continue	__continue
obey	__obey
encourage	__courage

NOTES: The blank represents one of the three negative prefixes, ***un-, mis-, dis-***. The challenge to the student is to choose the right one. The students can also be asked to identify the adjectives and verbs. In this game, ***dis-*** occurs with verbs (***continue, obey,*** and ***encourage***). Note that the prefix ***en-*** is dropped on ***encourage*** to make ***discourage***. Also note that ***place*** could be used with ***dis-***.

49

5.7 Synonyms A

beautiful	pretty
kind	helpful
silly	ridiculous
smart	intelligent
amusing	funny
unfortunate	unlucky
mad	angry
unhappy	sad
hard	difficult
ancient	very old
happy	cheerful
dull	boring

NOTES: When a match is made, the student should say, "X is similar to y." Then they can try to use one of the words in a sentence, and challenge another student to use the other word. This game may be a little easier than Synonyms B.

5.8 Synonyms B

shy	bashful
intentional	on purpose
take	accept
outstanding	excellent
hideous	ugly
positive	sure
evil	wicked
awkward	clumsy
weary	tired
marvelous	wonderful
clever	witty
enormous	huge

NOTES: When a match is made, the student should say, "X is similar to y." Then they can try to use one of the words in a sentence, and challenge another student to use the other word. This game may be a little harder than Synonyms A.

5.9 Antonyms A

hot	cold
long	short
old	young
ugly	beautiful
sad	happy
graceful	clumsy
quiet	noisy
large	small
dirty	clean
wide	narrow
sunrise	sunset
easy	difficult

NOTES: After the match has been made, the student should say, "X is the opposite of y." You could also ask them to make a sentence using both words and a *but*. For example, "Summer is **hot,** *but* winter is **cold.**"

5.10 Antonyms B

wet	dry
weak	strong
excited	calm
interesting	boring
mean	kind
light	heavy
tight	loose
open	closed
rich	poor
sharp	dull
full	empty
good	bad

NOTES: After the match has been made, the student should say, "*X* is the opposite of *y*." You could also ask them to make a sentence using both words and a **but**. For example, "Water is **wet**, **but** sand is **dry**."

WORDS 5

5.11 Participles as Modifiers

amazing	amazed
amusing	amused
boring	bored
interesting	interested
irritating	irritated
confusing	confused
disappointing	disappointed
disgusting	disgusted
embarrassing	embarrassed
exciting	excited
satisfying	satisfied
surprising	surprised

NOTES: The matches are easy to make, but using these participles as adjectives is not so easy. To work on this, the students can be required to make a sentence when they make the match. One possible sentence is "The (movie, etc.) was *X*ing and I was *Y*ed." This sentence could also include intensifiers "The (movie) was very/ really/ awfully/rather/ pretty/ extremely, *X*ing. . . ." You could even use the unusual exclamatory word order, ". . . and, man, was I ever *Y*ed."

5.12 Noun Suffixes

brother	-hood
friend	-ship
free	-dom
act	-ion
kind	-ness
prefer	-ence
critic	-ism
disappear	-ance
state	-ment
pack	-age
human	-ity
illiter-	-acy

NOTES: These matches employ almost all the common noun suffixes. Some spelling variations are not included. Thousands of nouns can be formed with this list of suffixes, and this particular set is only intended to introduce the students to the forms. After the game, you can have the students try to make lists of all the nouns they know that have these suffixes. You could give each pair of students a different suffix and see who wins the suffix championship (*-ion* will probably win).

5.13 Verb Affixes

en-	large
en-	courage
short	-en
sharp	-en
ident-	-ify
class	-ify
simpl-	-ify
critic	-ize
memor-	-ize
standard	-ize
liber-	-ate
toler-	-ate

NOTES: These matches employ almost all the common verb affixes. Note that **en** is both a prefix and suffix. Also note that there are only four common verb affixes, and for that reason, there are two or three matching combinations possible. This may make the game go a little faster, but be sure the students can use the words, as well as make the matches.

5.14 Adjective and Adverb Suffixes

origin	-al
gold	-en
reason	-able
cloud	-y
danger	-ous
prime	-ary
tickle	-ish
hero	-ic
attract	-ive
slow	-ly
to	-ward
clock	-wise

NOTES: The last three matches in this list are adverbs. Note that *-wards* is also an acceptable form, but *-ward* is the preferred current usage (*backwards* is an exception). Current usage also discourages the tendency to overuse *-wise*. Watch the spelling of *prime* and *tickle*. This list does not contain *-ful* or *-less*. To make the adjective list more complete, you can take one or two pairs from game 5.1. After the game, you can have the students try to make other adjectives by putting a suffix on the board for a rapid-fire brainstorm.

5.15 Agent Suffixes

foreign	-er
employ	-er
employ	-ee
inspect	-or
law	-yer
cash	-ier
engine	-eer
tour	-ist
econom-	-ist
immigr-	-ant
account	-ant
music	-ian

NOTES: There are thousands of agent nouns formed with these suffixes. This game only introduces the common forms. Note the *-er* and *-ee* contrast. You could have the students try to make more when the game is finished. Many nationality words are formed with variations of *-ian*. See game 4.2.

6.1 Food

potato	chips
french	fries
hot	dog
pan	cake
olive	oil
orange	juice
Swiss	cheese
water	melon
meat	ball
oat	meal
blue	berry
ice	cream

NOTES: These are all compound nouns and, as typical in compounds, all but one has the heaviest stress on the first syllable (Swiss Cheese). When the game is complete see if the students can find the "odd ball." Also note that some of these are traditionally spelled as one word, most as two. Have the students try to figure that out (One word: *oatmeal, pancake, watermelon, blueberry, meatball*). When a match is made, the student could be asked to declare whether they've ever had *X Y* or if they like or don't like *X Y*.

6.2 Food Collocations with 'n

bread	butter
salt	pepper
bacon	eggs
fish	chips
bacon, lettuce	tomato
milk	honey
sugar	spice
half	half
spaghetti	meatballs
pork	beans
soup	sandwich
meat	potatoes

NOTES: These collocations are typically spoken with the reduced 'n. They are always said in the order indicated above. For example, **not** *butter 'n bread*. Of course, it doesn't matter with *half 'n half*. So require the students to say the match with 'n and in the proper order. Some of the combos (*milk n' honey, sugar 'n spice*) are idiomatic, and don't refer to typical modern food combinations. This game should be played as a follow-up activity after the collocations have been introduced and explained.

6.3 Recreation

collect	stamps
watch	birds
climb	mountains
play	tennis
go	camping
read	books
listen to	music
grow	flowers
fly	kites
take	photos
ride	horses
catch	fish

NOTES: You should go over these collocations before playing the game because *collect,* for example, could occur with *books, music,* or *photos.* When a match is made, you could have the students say something like, "Many people like to *X Y,* and I do too/but I prefer *Z*/but I don't like to do that." You could also ask them to say the usual name of the person who does it. For example, *a bird watcher watches birds.* But be careful. In addition to the obvious, you could use *camper, book/music lover, gardener, photographer, horsewoman,* or *fisherman.*

6.4 Sportspeople

coach	coach
runner	run
sprinter	sprint
skater	skate
skiier	ski
boxer	box
wrestler	wrestle
surfer	surf
swimmer	swim
diver	dive
jogger	jog
bowler	bowl

NOTES: These matches are fairly obvious. After the match is made, the students should say, "A *x* *y*s," or "*X*s *y*." For example, "Joggers jog." To add to the fun, have them use an appropriate adjective and adverb from this list: *careful, fast, good, clever, brave, cheerful, happy, successful, nervous.* The student would say, "A clever coach coaches cleverly." Watch out for *fast* and *good.*

COMPOUNDS & COLLOCATIONS

6.5 Sports

weight	lifting
table	tennis
volley	ball
field	hockey
pole	vaulting
long	jumping
figure	skating
jai	alai
auto	racing
hang	gliding
wind	surfing
platform	diving

NOTES: When a match is made, you could have the students say something like, "Some people like *x* , but I would rather ...." This could be tricky since the verb could be "*play, watch, do.*" You could also have the students name the person who does this sport. Be careful. For the games, we say an *x player*. The athletes doing the other sports are called *x-er*. For example, we say a *jai alai player* but a *long jumper*. This could be followed by "A weight lifter lifts weights," or "A pole vaulter vaults," practicing the third person ending.

6.6 Using Vehicles

ride	bicycle
ride	horse
row	boat
paddle	canoe
fly	plane
drive	truck
drive	car
push	baby carriage
tow	trailer
pilot	tug boat
operate	elevator
pull	wagon

NOTES: Various combinations are possible in this set, but finding and using the most common collocation is the point. You could try this: name the vehicle and have the students try to use the appropriate verb. After the collocations have been identified, play the game. Afterward, you could have the students use passive constructions. For example, "Bicycles are ridden."

6.7 Car and Driver

driver's	license
parking	ticket
pedestrian	crossing
snow	tires
full/self	serve
hand	brake
rear-view	mirror
gas	tank
stop	sign
one	way
passing	lane
dead	end

NOTES: This game, and the one that follows could supplement a unit on getting a license or learning to drive. Have the students explain the collocated forms when they make a match. A review of road signs would also be useful.

6.8 Driving

wash and wax	the car
run over	an animal
shift into	reverse
run out of	gas
stop, look, and	listen
fill it	up
change	the oil
have	a flat tire
dim	the lights
buckle	the seat belt
obey	the speed limit
slow	down

NOTES: All of these matches start with a verb. When a match is made, the students can try to put the verb into the past. They can also use the verb in one of these sentences: "I hope I don't ..., I wish you would ..., I think I should ...." This game can be played in conjunction with the preceding game.

6.9 Tools

hammer	pounding nails
saw	cutting wood
screwdriver	turning screws
sandpaper	sanding wood
file	filing
drill	drilling holes
paint brush	painting
wrench	turning nuts
axe	chopping wood
tape measure	measuring
planer	planing
broom	cleaning up

NOTES: The tools may be new to the student, and so illustrations might be helpful. The key sentence for making the match is, "A *x* is used for *y*." For example, "An axe is used for chopping wood." You could also do, "For *y*ing, you need a *x*," "To *y*, you need a *x*."

6.10 Containers, Packages, etc.

tube	toothpaste
loaf	bread
pack	gum
six-pack	beer
pound	hamburger
bag	potatoes
quart	milk
bunch	bananas
roll	toilet paper
dozen	eggs
head	lettuce
stick	butter

NOTES: The matches can be made with a sentence such as, "I need a x of y." For example, "stick of butter." You could also do, "I bought two x(s) of y." Watch out for the irregular *loaves, bunches,* and *dozen* – "six dozen eggs." The products also illustrate countable and uncountable nouns, and this could lead to a flash card game where the key phrase is "a lot of" and the product on the card is in the singular form – you can copy and white-out the plural *s* in the examples above and make more product names of your own. For example, you flash *egg* and the student responds with, "I bought *a lot of egg*s," and if you flash *lettuce,* the response is, "I bought *a lot of lettuce*." You could also do, "I didn't buy much/many y."

6.11 Computerese

back	up
down	load
print	out
save	as
empty	trash
log	on
chat	room
mega	byte
hard	drive
start up	disk
surf	the net
cut	paste

NOTES: Since there is a lot of variation in the forms of these expressions, it will be best to go over them first. Some are verbs, some nouns, and **back up, down load,** and **print out** can be both. Note the collocation **cut and paste.** After the matches have been made, the students can ask and answer questions such as, "Tell me the meaning of *x (surf the net).*" With the verbs, the students can ask "Do you know how to *x (log on),*" or "Do you like *xing (logging on).*" With nouns, "Do you have a new *x (hard drive).*"

6.12 Animal Sounds

dog	bark
duck	quack
rooster	crow
cat	meow
owl	hoot
pig	grunt
cow	moo
horse	neigh
hen	cluck
lion	roar
mouse	squeak
frog	croak

NOTES: In addition to the matches, it is always fun to compare the sounds that the same animal makes in different languages. In addition to making the match, the students can try to make the sound itself. The match can be made with either "*xs y*" or "A *x y*s." This is a good practice for the moving *s,* as in, "Dog*s* bark," and "A dog bark*s.*"

6.13 Animal Babies

cow	calf
lion	cub
sheep	lamb
horse	colt
goat	kid
pig	piglet
deer	fawn
goose	gosling
cat	kitten
duck	duckling
dog	puppy
hen	chick

NOTES: When the match is made, the student says, "A baby *x* is a y,'" or "Baby *x*s are *y*s." For example, "A baby goose is a gosling." In the latter sentence, watch out for the irregular ***sheep, deer, goose***.

7.1 Similes with *as* • Animals

sly	fox
strong	ox
busy	bee
slippery	eel
free	bird
blind	bat
crazy	loon
wise	owl
happy	clam
proud	peacock
stubborn	mule
silly	goose

NOTES: These matches are completed with the phrase "as *x* as a *y*." For example, "She's as wise an owl." After the game, you can have an interesting discussion about the characteristics of these animals as seen in English and on how other cultures view these animals.

7.2 Similes with *like*

work	dog
drink	fish
sleep	log
drive	maniac
eat	pig
run	deer
hop	bunny
cry	baby
roar	lion
purr	kitten
smell	rose
sing	angel

NOTES: These matches are completed with the phrase "*x* like a *y*." For example, "The wind roared like a lion." The meanings of these expressions will require some explanation, but making sentences with the subject pronouns *he/she/it* would be fairly easy. For example, "He cries like a baby."

7.3 More Similes

high	kite
easy	pie
cool	cucumber
old	hills
pretty	picture
dead	doornail
nutty	fruitcake
sober	judge
naked	jaybird
flat	pancake
American	apple pie
bright	button

NOTES: Some of the vocabulary here is unusual, and so it will probably be necessary to spend some time defining and explaining these words. The matches are completed with the phrase "as *x* as a *y*." For example, "as cool as a cucumber. Note "as easy as pie" and "as old as *the* hills" are exceptions. After the game, the students can try to decide who or what is described by the similes.

7.4 Collocated Pairs with Nouns

do's	don'ts
brothers	sisters
ladies	gentlemen
odds	ends
cops	robbers
cowboys	indians
aches	pains
thunder	lightning
supply	demand
sticks	stones
fame	fortune
husband	wife

NOTES: These expressions are said in the order they appear above. For example, "do's" before "don'ts," not "don'ts and do's." This game could probably be done without first going through the meanings of the expressions because the matches are fairly obvious. What else, other than *robbers* would go with *cops*? After the game, the meaning and usage could be explored.

7.5 Collocated Pairs with *and* A

up	down
over	done with
lost	found
stop	go
off	on
back	forth
forever	ever
nice	easy
rise	shine
out	out
safe	sound
time	again

NOTES: These pairs are not easy. It might be advisable to prepare a handout of 12 sentences that use the expressions, and then to go over them with the students before playing the game.

7.6 Collocated Pairs with *and* B

up	coming
straight	narrow
over	over
now	forever
first	foremost
hard	fast
each	every
far	away
wear	tear
sick	tired
fun	games
hit	run

NOTES: These pairs are not easy, and so it might be advisable to prepare a handout of 12 sentences that use the expressions, and then to go over them with the students before playing the game.

7.7 Collocated Pairs with *and* C

more	more
few	far between
front	center
hot	bothered
betwixt	between
down	out
fast	furious
spick	span
tried	true
pure	simple
rough	tumble
high	mighty

NOTES: These pairs are possibly the most difficult of the three sets of this type, and so it would be advisable to prepare a handout of 12 sentences that use the expressions and then to go over them with the students before playing the game.

7.8 Collocated Pairs with *or*

ifs, ands	buts
dead	alive
friend	foe
on	about
right	wrong
feast	famine
plus	minus
give	take
more	less
ready	not
hit	miss
do	die

NOTES: These pairs are tricky. It may be helpful to prepare a pre-game activity using the phrases in example sentences.

7.9 Adjective Pairs

wide	awake
stir	crazy
red	hot
freezing	cold
sound	asleep
bone	dry
slap	happy
razor	sharp
dirt	cheap
picture	perfect
bare	naked
hard	hit

NOTES: These expressions will require some pre-game work. Example sentences would be useful. You could also have the students make a sentence with either "I was *x y (I was stir crazy),*" or "It was *x y.*" In some cases, both will work, but in others, only one works.

7.10 Collocated Pairs with *Of*

cream	crop
proof	pudding
time	life
out	woods
talk	town
slip	tongue
tip	iceberg
hard	hearing
month	Sundays
word	mouth
end	rope
act	God

NOTES: Some of these pairs require a determiner. The students should give the complete expression when they make a match. *Life* and *rope* require possessive adjectives.

7.11 Triplets

knife	fork	spoon
tall	dark	handsome
love	honor	obey
beg	borrow	steal
healthy	wealthy	wise
lock	stock	barrel
win	place	show
ready	willing	able
hop	skip	jump
stop	look	listen
morning	noon	night
eat	drink	be merry

NOTES: This game requires 36 cards. The students should have three guesses as they try to match the three parts of the triplets. Two of these triplets are connected by *or*. Also notice that the order in which the three words are said is fixed. For example, "fork, spoon and knife" is not said.

8.1 Idioms A • Food

to bring home	the bacon
the cream	of the crop
two peas	in a pod
sour	grapes
to spill	the beans
square	meal
to take	the cake
half	baked
hard	boiled
watered	down
to not know	beans about (something)
to take something	with a grain of salt

NOTES: Idioms are not easy. It would be best to go over the list with the students before playing the game. When they make a match, they should also try to use the idiom in a sentence.

8.2 Idioms B • House and Home

to hit	home
on	the house
to raise	the roof
wet	blanket
to turn	the tables
to pull up	stakes
to make oneself	at home
household	word
room	and board
to bring down	the house
house	warming
home	coming

NOTES: Idioms are not easy. It would be best to go over the list with the students before playing the game. When they make a match, they should also try to use the idiom in a sentence. The last two pairs are compound nouns spelled as one word.

all	ears
to bend over	backwards
in cold	blood
to waste	one's breath
to get cold	feet
to cool	one's heels
to rub	elbows
to see	eye to eye
to shake	a leg
slip	of the tongue
narrow	minded
to let down	one's hair

NOTES: There are many more idioms associated with the body. After the game, you can ask the students if they have heard others. After the match has been made, the students should try to use the idioms in a sentence.

8.4 Idioms D • Health

black	and blue
to catch	a cold
a pain	in the neck
sick	and tired
a sight	for sore eyes
safe	and sound
hard	of hearing
over	the hill
to have	a screw loose
to kick	the bucket
dead	as a doornail
one foot	in the grave

NOTES: Although all these idioms allude to health, their figurative meanings may be a little different. After the match has been made, the students should try to use the idioms in a sentence. For variety, you could ask them to write sentences. Check them over and put some of the sentences on poster paper. Make them aware that many of these idioms are very informal, and should not be used in formal writing.

8.5 Idioms E • The Environment

to break	the ice
to shoot	the breeze
to weather	the storm
a stick	in the mud
once	in a blue moon
a stone's	throw
dirt	cheap
to blow off	steam
up the creek	without a paddle
to bog	down
the tip	of an iceberg
to knock	on wood

NOTES: Although all these idioms allude to the natural world, their figurative meanings may be a little different. Try going over the environmental terms for meaning and then let the students play the game. They should be able to guess many of the matches correctly.

8.6 Proverbs A • Food

than none.	is better	Half a loaf
of life.	is the spice	Variety
the broth.	spoil	Too many cooks
that feeds you.	the hand	Don't bite
spilled milk.	over	Don't cry
served.	first	First come
the fire.	and into	Out of the frying pan
and have it, too.	your cake	You can't eat

NOTES: Proverbs are usually full sentences. Because they are longer, the proverb games are set up in three columns. They are best played by setting up a three-column grid with eight rows. Mix the cards within each column, but do not mix the cards from one column to another. The players should have three guesses, one for each column with each turn. The proverbs may be transparent enough to play the game without much preview activity, other than telling the players the literal meaning is about food and cooking.

8.7 Proverbs B • Animals

His bark	is worse	than his bite.
You can't teach	an old dog	new tricks.
When the cat's away	the mice	will play.
Don't look	a gift horse	in the mouth.
The early bird	catches	the worm.
A bird in the hand	is worth	two in the bush.
Birds of a feather	flock	together.
Don't count	your chickens	before they hatch.

NOTES: Proverbs are usually full sentences. Because they are longer, the proverb games are set up in three columns. They are best played by setting up a three-column grid with eight rows. Mix the cards within each column, but do not mix the cards from one column to another. The players should have three guesses, one for each column with each turn. The proverbs may be transparent enough to play the game without much preview activity, other than telling the players the literal meaning is about animals.

8.8 Proverbs C • Advice

He	who hesitates	is lost.
Honesty	is	the best policy.
Haste	makes	waste.
Beggars	can't be	choosers.
Actions	speak louder	than words.
Spare the rod	and spoil	the child.
Don't throw out	the baby	with the bath water.
Rome	wasn't built	in a day.

NOTES: Proverbs are usually full sentences. Because they are longer, the proverb games are set up in three columns. They are best played by setting up a three-column grid with eight rows. Mix the cards within each column, but do not mix the cards from one column to another. The players should have three guesses, one for each column with each turn. The proverbs may be transparent enough to play the game without much preview activity. However, if you think the game will be too challenging, turn all the cards in the last column over so that one-third of the proverb is visible. Then the players get two guesses, one for each of the first two columns.

8.9 Proverbs D • Miscellaneous

A penny saved	is	a penny earned.
Children	should be seen	and not heard.
When in Rome	do	as the Romans do.
Absence	makes the heart	grow fonder.
Beauty	is only	skin deep.
If the shoe	fits	wear it.
Blood	is thicker	than water.
Don't judge	a book	by its cover.

NOTES: Proverbs are usually full sentences. Because they are longer, the proverb games are set up in three columns. They are best played by setting up a three-column grid with eight rows. Mix the cards within each column, but do not mix the cards from one column to another. The players should have three guesses, one for each column with each turn. You may need to go over these proverbs before the playing the game. One way is to call out the words in the first column, and see if the students know or can guess the remainder of the proverb. An alternative is to begin the game with all the cards in the last column face up.

Other Books of Interest from Pro Lingua

Index Card Games for ESL — A collection of seven language games. This is a photocopyable teacher resource that tells how to play each game and provides samples for beginning, intermediate, and advanced students.

More Index Card Games — Nine more photocopyable games that use index cards. Sample games are provided at appropriate levels.

The Great Big BINGO Book — 44 photocopyable games practice vocabulary, grammar, pronunciation, writing, and cultural information.

The Great Big Book of Crosswords — 60 photocopyable games build vocabulary through individual, pair, and triad work.

Solo, Duo, Trio — 118 photocopyable puzzles and games for individuals, pairs, or triads build vocabulary, spelling, and reading skills.

Pronunciation Card Games — Index card games that focus on pronunciation. Practicing minimal pairs, stress placement, rhythm, and intonation is fun and lively with these games.

Shenanigames — 49 photocopyable grammar-focused games.

Discovery Trail — a board game with 900 question cards on ten topics: Grammar (x3), prepostions, phrasal verbs, idioms, proverbs, US and world history and geography, and US citizenship.

Surveys for Conversation — Students read and write answers to 48 surveys preparing to talk about family, friendship, pets, shopping, TV, music, computers, space, celebrations, love, marriage, birth & death, work, books, health, crime, war & peace, 2100 AD, and the environment.

The ESL Miscellany — A copyable teacher resource book that contains lots of lists with thousands of words that can be consulted for making index card games. There are also lists of grammar points, cultural information, communicative functions, situations, and 60 topical lists — a frequent source for the games in **Match It!**

www.Pro Lingua Associates.com • 800-366-4775